Boost Your Brand with Alexa and WordPress

Voice Branding in Under 30 Minutes

by

Nigel Creaser

two7four

PUBLISHING

Copyright © 2019 Nigel Creaser

All rights reserved.

If the eagle eyed among you spot a typo, please let me know by dropping me an email with the subject **Typo Alert** to typo@two7four.com.

Table of Contents

Chapter 1

Introduction

What does this book aim to do?

Hi, and welcome, this guide aims to provide a quick (under 30 minutes), cheap and easily accessible set of instructions to create a voice experience attached to your brand for your customers. We will do this by creating an Alexa Flash Briefing skill which is linked to a WordPress.com site. In the interest of being quick and simple I have kept the explanations of what is on the screen and why it is there to a minimum, my aim really is to allow you to have it all created in under 30 minutes, so if some of the pages are just click the continue button, that's why.

Another point to mention is that the rate of change and enhancements to the platform by Amazon is very rapid so some of the pages may look different or other features may be introduced. If something does not work, just drop me an email with the subject line "**Something is bust**" to help@two7four.com and I will see if I can help.

What it is not?

It will **not,** let me reiterate **NOT** teach you how to code Alexa skills, if your goal is to do this, there are vast resources on the internet, the Alexa development portal has a great many features and tutorials that will provide you all the information you need.

It will, however provide you with an introduction to some of the Alexa concepts and show how to quickly set up an Alexa Flash Briefing skill which will allow your customers to start interacting with your brand, using the Amazon Alexa platform and all the devices that hang off it.

Who is it aimed at?

It is intended for individuals and organisations like yours wishing to take your first steps on the path to engaging with your customers using the voice capabilities of the Alexa devices, but who do not have an army of coding and voice designers, or extremely deep pockets to pay a software house to create it for you.

You do not need any coding experience to follow the instructions in this book, the main skills required are curiosity and ability to follow instructions, at this point please do not go to Appendix X yet we have a few other things to discuss.

What is Alexa?

In purchasing this book I assume you know what Alexa is, that being said let's make sure we are all on the same page of the hymn book, starting off on the right foot, have all our ducks in a row,[insert your management phrase of choice].

Alexa is Amazon's framework for dealing with voice interactions, sometimes called a voice assistant sometimes called an AI (artificial intelligence) and is similar to other tooling including Google Assistant, Apple's Siri, Microsoft's Cortana or Samsung's Bixby.

Alexa is accessed primarily via one of a number of Amazon Echo devices, 3rd party suppliers like Sonos and Marshall or the Alexa smartphone app.

Alexa allows users to use their voice to request information, control household devices such as lighting, play music or manage shopping lists, to name but a few. More capability coming online very regularly.

What are Skills?

The simplest explanation I can give is that if you think of your smart speaker as a smart phone, then the skills are like the apps on your phone. Amazon has created Alexa Skills Kit which allows developers to extend and enhance the functionality of the Alexa service, by creating Skills. This means organisations can use this new channel for marketing purposes, retailing, customer support, entertainment etc. Very much like the smartphone apps ecosystem the limitations are really only in the imaginations of the developers.

What is a Flash Briefing?

Included with in the Alexa command set is the concept of a Flash Briefing providing a way in which your customers can ask Alexa for news that is tailored specifically for their interest, this is achieved by them enabling a skill from the Alexa Skill store, very similar to apps store or google play and also allows organisations to create a flash briefing skill that can be plugged into the users daily briefing.

The skills store is accessed by either searching in the Amazon store under skill or via the Alexa phone app or by even asking Alexa for a skill for a specific purpose.

What Will I Learn?

During this tutorial you will learn:

- how to create an Amazon Developer Account

- how to create WordPress.com account

- how to create WordPress.com site to hold the content of your briefing and some basic content

- how to create an Alexa Flash Briefing Skill linked to your content in the WordPress.com site.

Chapter 2

Create your Amazon Developer Account

Firstly open up your web browser of choice, I tend to use Google Chrome but this should work fine with most other browsers too, though the way in looks on the page may vary slightly.

Navigate to the https://developer.amazon.com.

Click on the **"Sign In"** link.

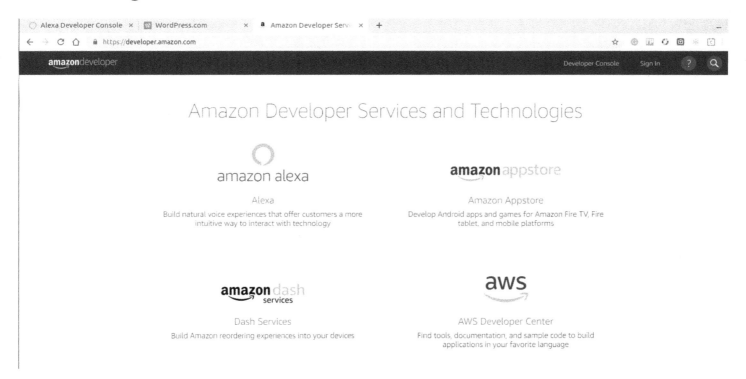

Click on the **"Create your Amazon Developer account"** button.

Fill in your details and decide on a password. At this point if you have an Amazon Echo device already registered to an email address you may consider using the same email address for the developer account, by doing this it will allow you to try out your skill when they are still under development. Not entirely necessary but something to consider. Then click **"Create your Amazon Developer account"**.

You will now be presented with the following screen, which is to make sure you a real person and not one of those pesky robots.

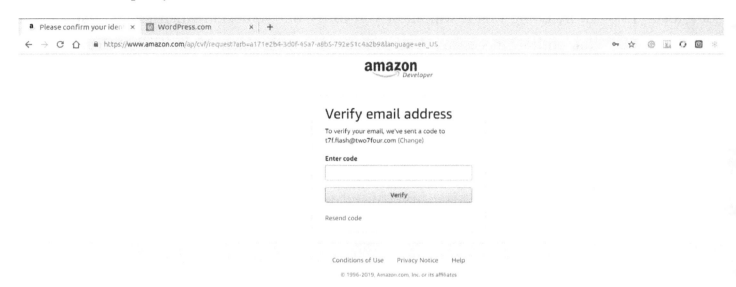

Pop over to your email and get the code, the email should look something like this.

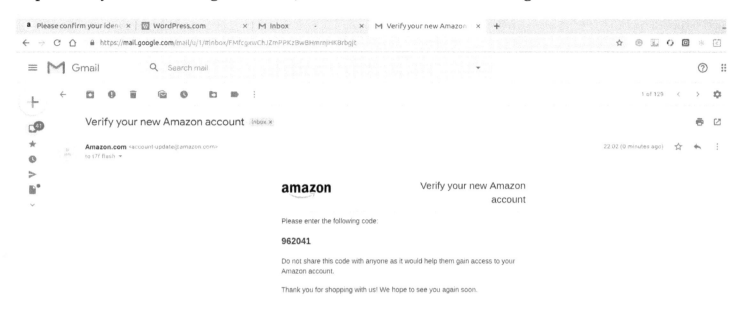

Enter the code and hit verify.

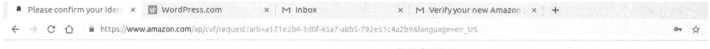

Verify email address

To verify your email, we've sent a code to
t7f.flash@two7four.com (Change)

Enter code

Verify

Resend code

Conditions of Use   Privacy Notice   Help

© 1996-2019, Amazon.com, Inc. or its affiliates

Enter the relevant details into the form, don't forget to scroll down.

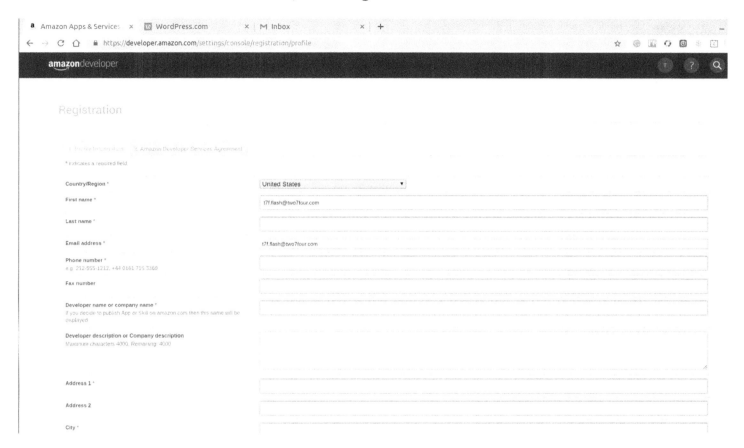

When you have completed the fields click **"Save and Continue"**.

Read, you will need to scroll down to see it all the details.

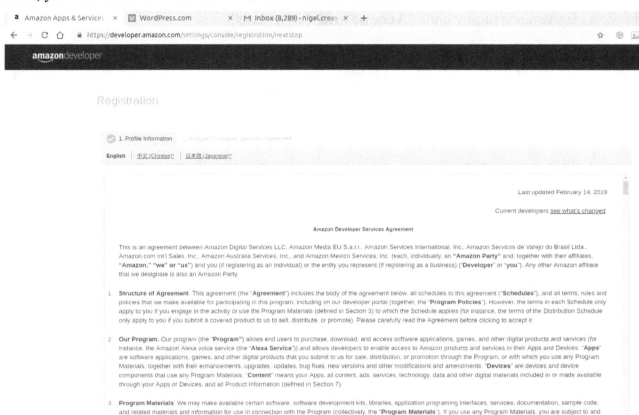

Registration

1. Profile Information

English | 中文 (Chinese)* | 日本語 (Japanese)*

Last updated February 14, 2019

Current developers see what's changed

Amazon Developer Services Agreement

This is an agreement between Amazon Digital Services LLC, Amazon Media EU S.a.r.l., Amazon Services International, Inc., Amazon Servicos de Varejo do Brasil Ltda., Amazon.com Int'l Sales, Inc., Amazon Australia Services, Inc., and Amazon Mexico Services, Inc. (each, individually, an **"Amazon Party"** and, together with their affiliates, **"Amazon," "we" or "us"**) and you (if registering as an individual) or the entity you represent (if registering as a business) (**"Developer"** or **"you"**). Any other Amazon affiliate that we designate is also an Amazon Party.

1. **Structure of Agreement**. This agreement (the "**Agreement**") includes the body of the agreement below, all schedules to this agreement ("**Schedules**"), and all terms, rules and policies that we make available for participating in this program, including on our developer portal (together, the "**Program Policies**"). However, the terms in each Schedule only apply to you if you engage in the activity or use the Program Materials (defined in Section 3) to which the Schedule applies (for instance, the terms of the Distribution Schedule only apply to you if you submit a covered product to us to sell, distribute, or promote). Please carefully read the Agreement before clicking to accept it.

2. **Our Program**. Our program (the "**Program**") allows end users to purchase, download, and access software applications, games, and other digital products and services (for instance, the Amazon Alexa voice service (the "**Alexa Service**")) and allows developers to enable access to Amazon products and services in their Apps and Devices. "**Apps**" are software applications, games, and other digital products that you submit to us for sale, distribution, or promotion through the Program, or with which you use any Program Materials, together with their enhancements, upgrades, updates, bug fixes, new versions and other modifications and amendments. "**Devices**" are devices and device components that use any Program Materials. "**Content**" means your Apps, all content, ads, services, technology, data and other digital materials included in or made available through your Apps or Devices, and all Product Information (defined in Section 7).

3. **Program Materials**. We may make available certain software, software development kits, libraries, application programing interfaces, services, documentation, sample code, and related materials and information for use in connection with the Program (collectively, the "**Program Materials**"). If you use any Program Materials, you are subject to and agree to comply with our Program Materials License Agreement (the "**Program Materials License**"), located at https://developer.amazon.com/support/legal/pml. Your use of

17

Once you have read and scrolled all the way down then you may want to print a copy, here is where you can do so. Once you are happy click "**Accept and Continue**".

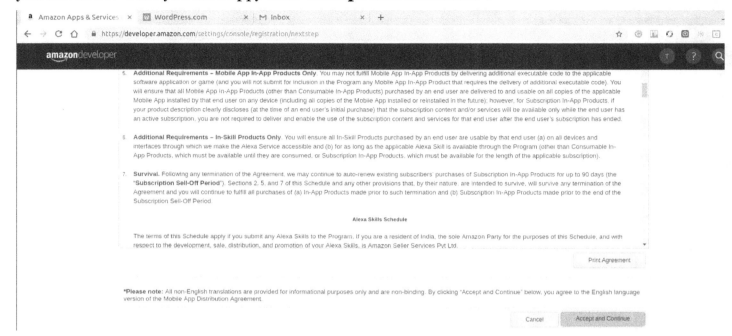

Congratulations! Your Amazon developer account has been created. Well done!

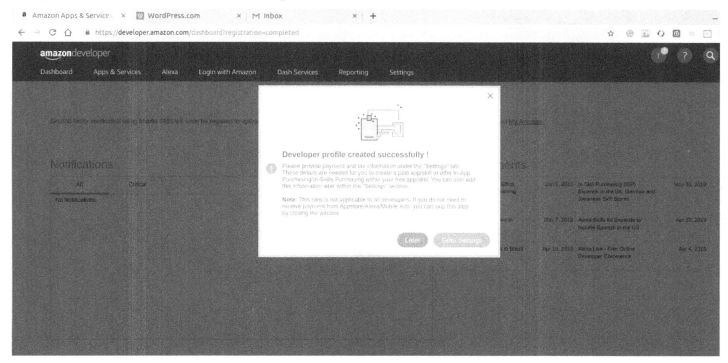

20

Chapter 3

Create Your WordPress.com Account and Site

We are now going to set up a WordPress.com account to allow you to create the WordPress.com site. Open a new tab in your browser or a new window, whichever you prefer.

Type the following in the address bar https://wordpress.com/create/?aff=9725 (just for awareness this is an affiliate link. That means, that if in the future, you decide to take up a paid subscription from WordPress.com, I will get a little something for referring you.)

Click the **"Get Started"** link.

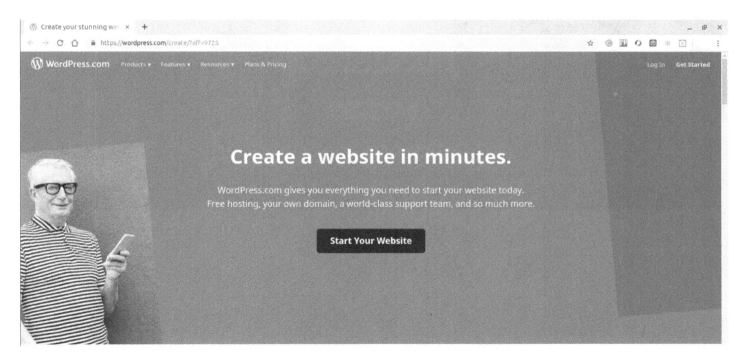

If you already have a WordPress user account then log in if not click "**Create your account**" or if you prefer to use Google click one "**Connect with Google**" button. For the purposes of this guide we will use the same email address we used for our Amazon developer account.

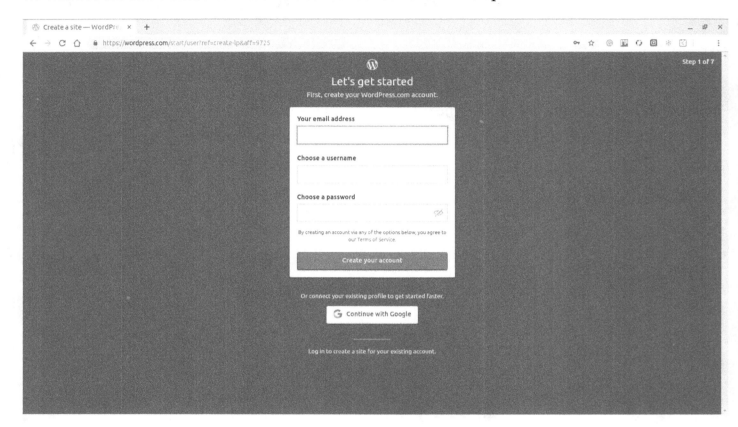

Fill out you email address and choose a user name, what ever you want, then choose a password.

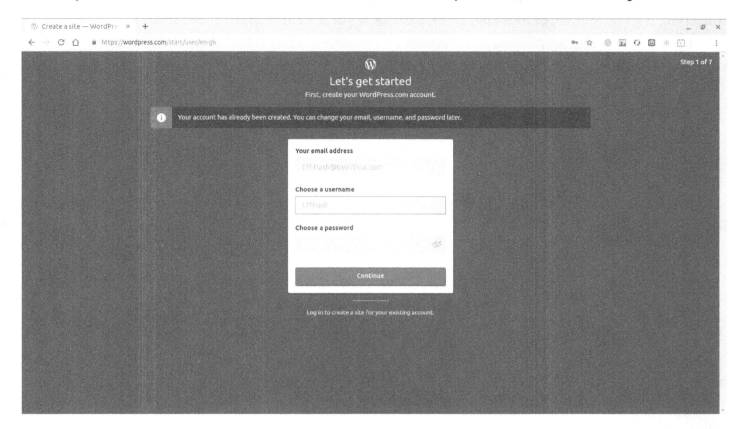

Next WordPress will ask you what kind of site you are planning to build. The choice will give you different type of templates and suggestions for how you might want a site to look, for our purposes we just want a simple blog so click on **"Blog".**

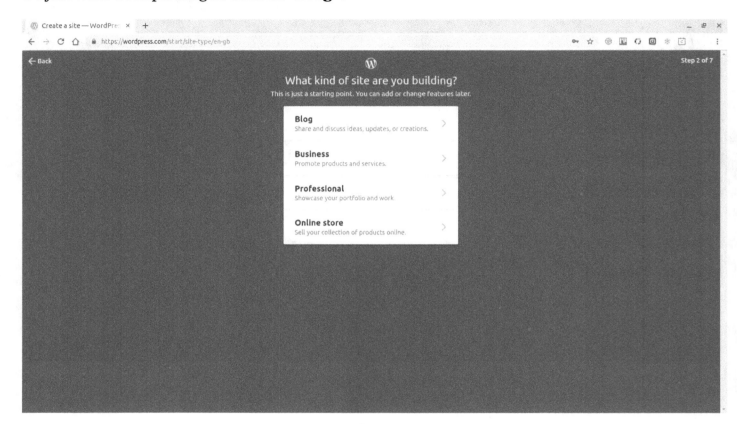

This screen again just helps WordPress decide what templates to show you and classify your site. Choose which ever seems appropriate to your skill. I am going to choose "**Food**".

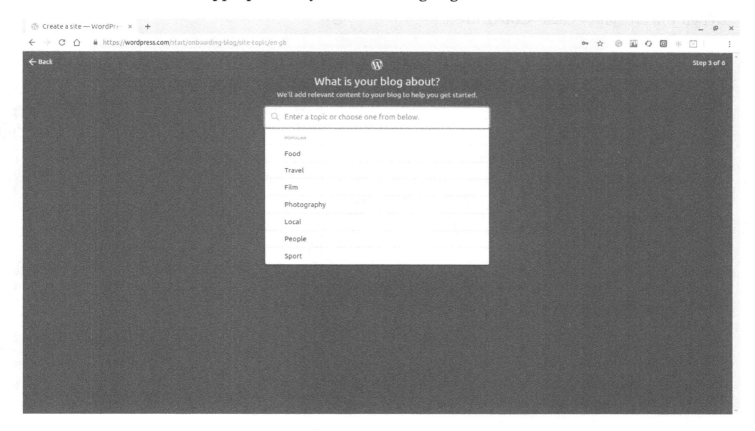

After you have clicked on your choice a "**Continue**" button will appear with your choice next to it. Click on it if you are happy, if you are not happy just click in the white text box and change it. When you are happy click "**Continue**".

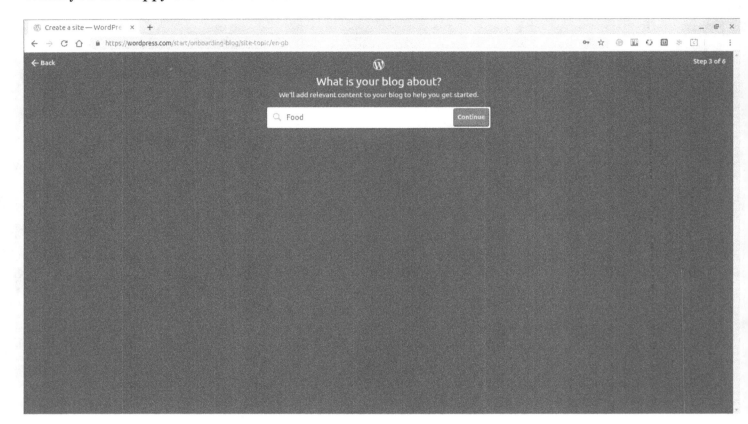

You will now be asked for a name for your site, it can be what ever you want. When you are happy click on "**Continue**".

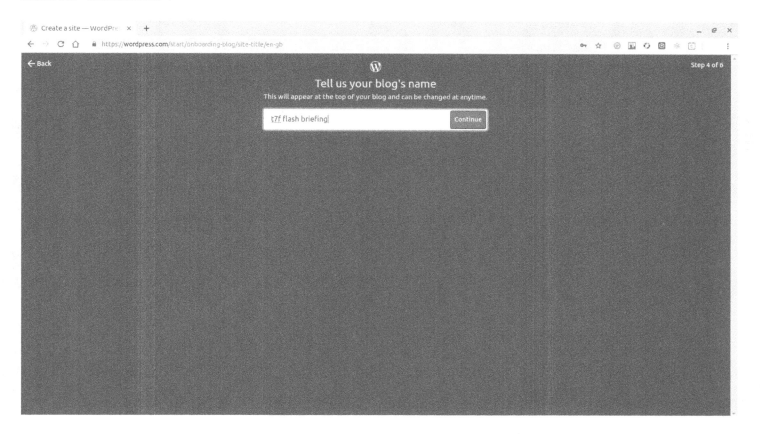

Now you can decide what the web address will be for your site. Again choose what you want, as you enter your text the screen will change showing you some options.

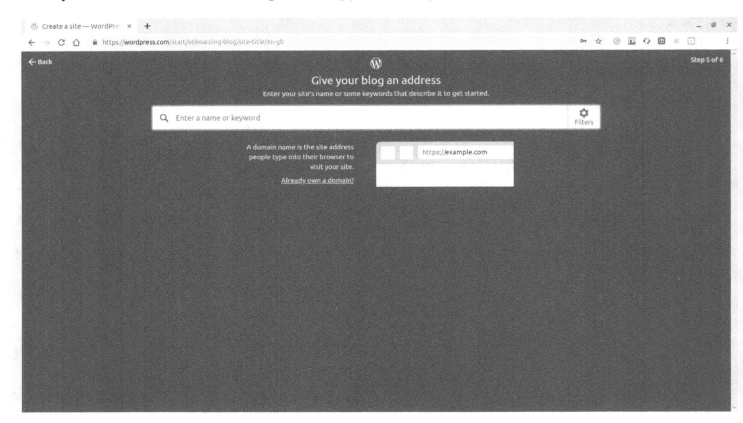

On this page be sure to click on the line that says "**FREE**".

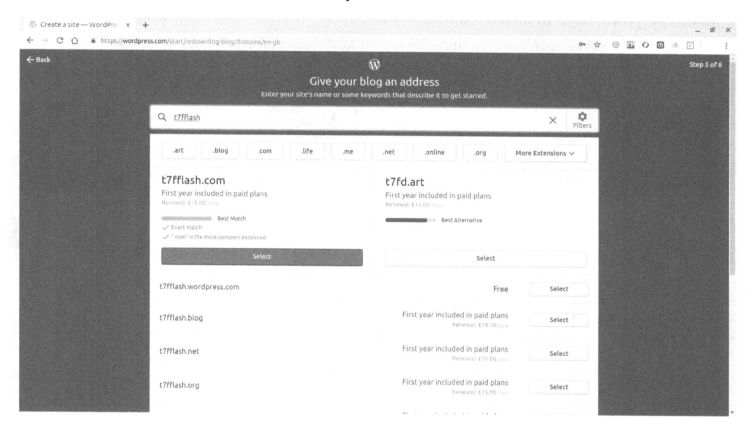

Here WordPress are trying to get you to sign up to one of their paid services, this is not necessary for our purposes, but if in future you wish to you can do. You will notice the inconspicuous option of "**Start with a free site**" as blue underlined text at the top of the screen. Click there.

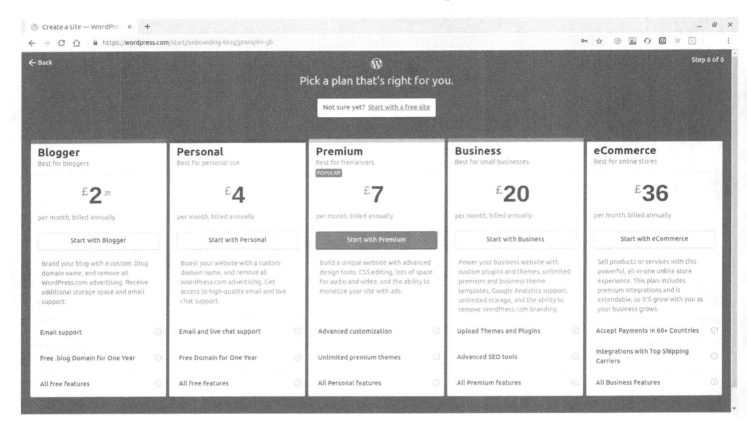

Hurrah, you have now created your site.

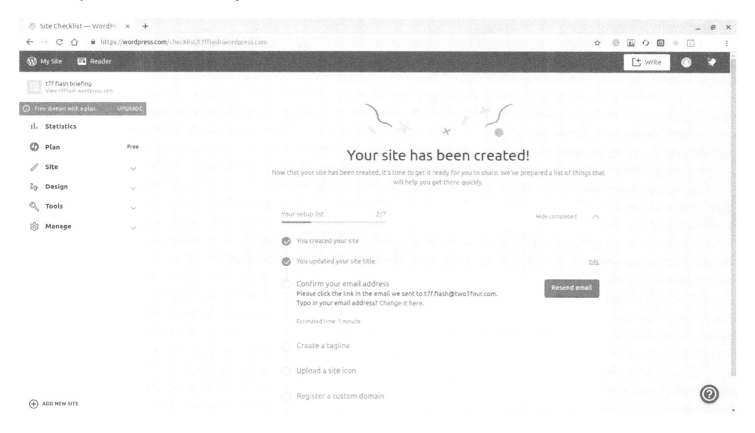

Log into your email and you should have an email that looks something like the one shown below. Press the **"Click here to Confirm Now"** button, and follow the instructions.

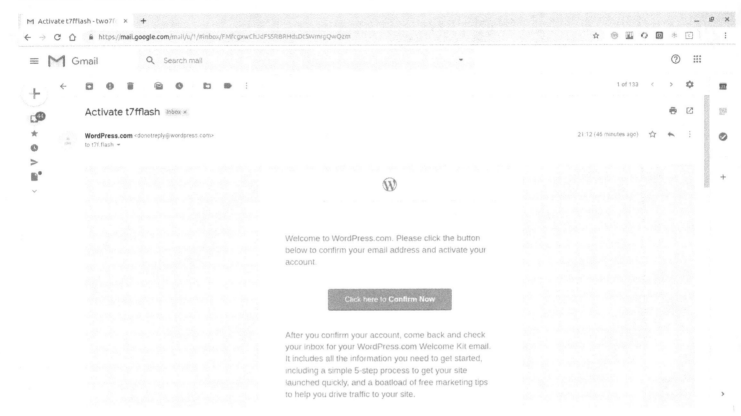

When you click on the link in the email you will see the following page. The remaining items are not necessary for our needs so we will move on to creating some content in your site to allow Alexa to read it out for you. See you in the next chapter.

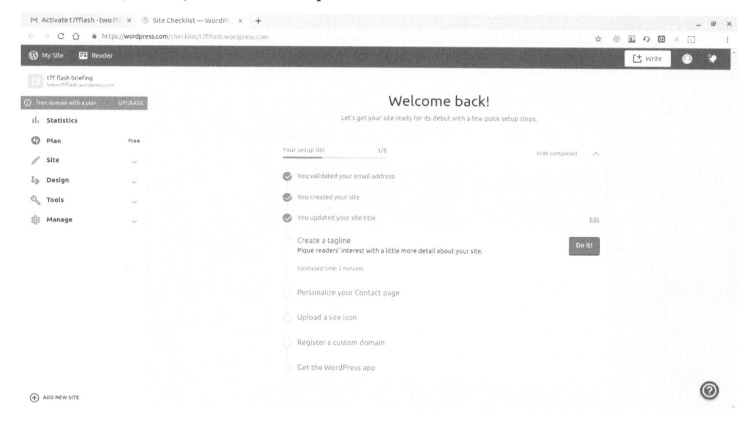

Chapter 4

Configure Your WordPress.com Site

Now we have created the bare bones of your site lets configure it so it works in the manner we want it to.

You should have received another email after you confirmed your site welcoming you to WordPress.com scroll down.

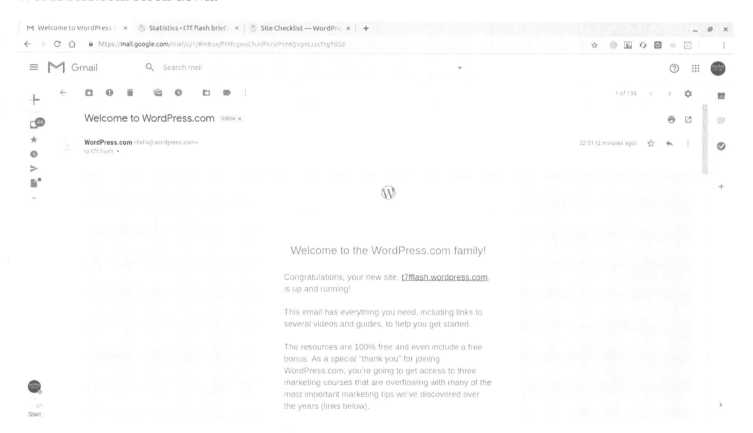

There will be a button that say something like **"Log in to WordPress.com"** click the button.

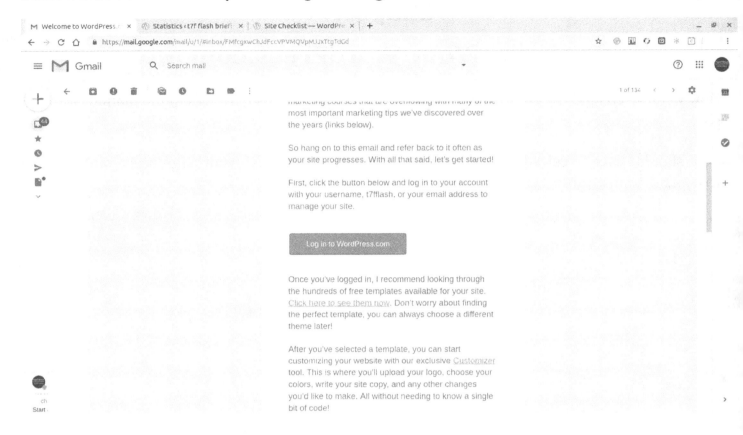

You should see the following screen. Click on "**Design**" and then "**Customise**".

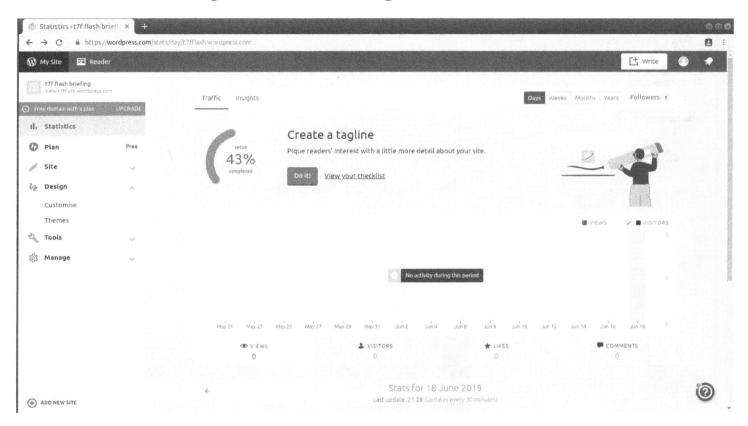

Click on **"Content Options"**.

Make sure that the "**Full Post**" radio button is checked, if you decide to change the theme in WordPress.com at all just check this setting is still set to **"Full Post"**. This makes sure that all of your content is available for Alexa to read out. Now click on the arrow pointing to the left of **"Content Options"**.

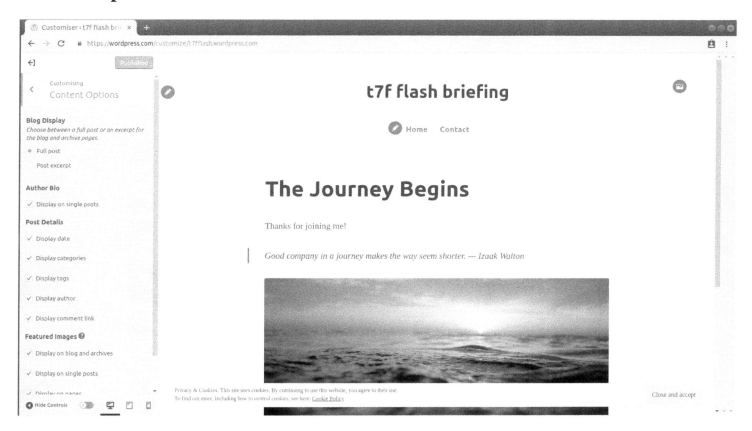

Click on the ⇤ next to published.

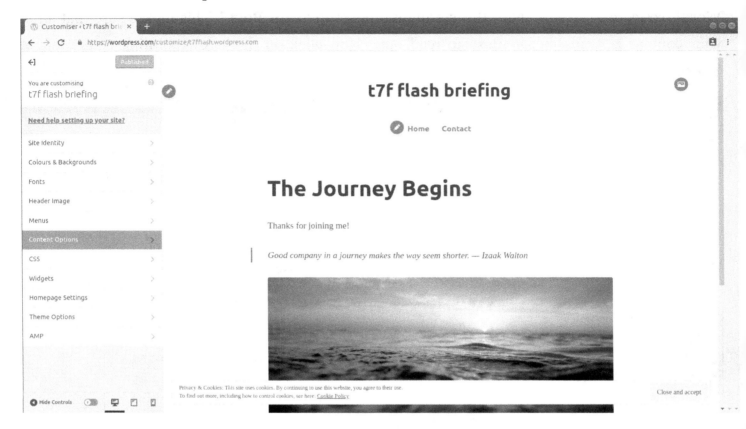

When you return the previous screen click on **"Manage"**, then on "**Settings**".

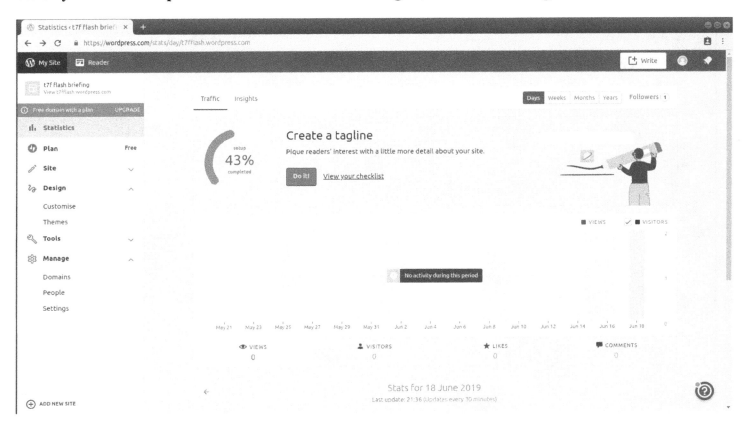

Click on the tab headed "**Writing**".

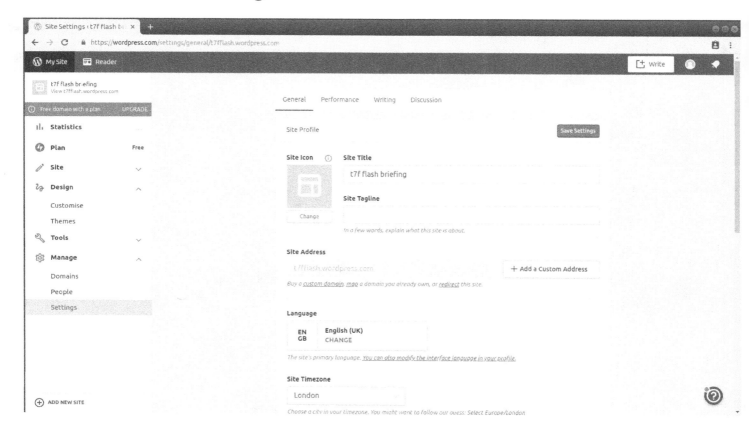

Scroll down the main section of the page until you see feed settings.

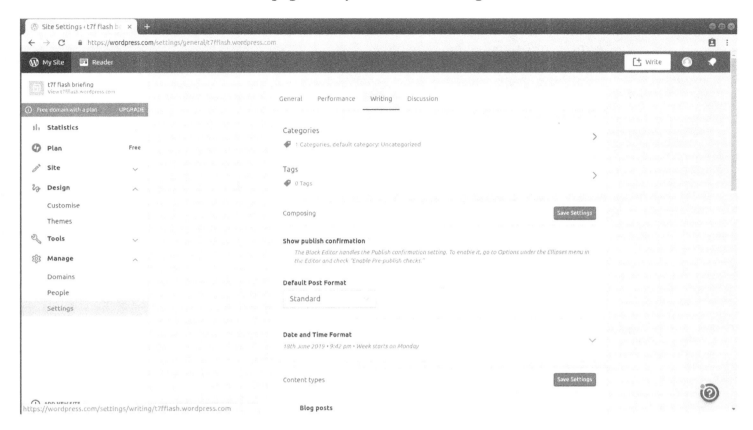

Change **"Display 10 most recent posts"** to **"Display 1 most recent posts"** and click **"Save settings"**.

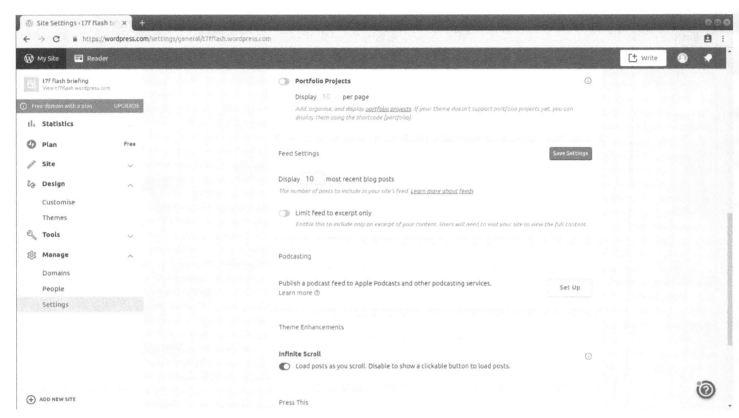

This means that Alexa will only read out one of your posts, having more than this is possible but you may annoy your listeners if your Flash Briefing takes too long and there is a 4500 character limit and it is cut off to the nearest sentence before that. In my experience your listener will lose interest way before that. For further details have a look here:

https://developer.amazon.com/docs/flashbriefing/flash-briefing-skill-api-feed-reference.html

Your site is now configured, we will now move on to creating some content for the site, click on **"My Site".**

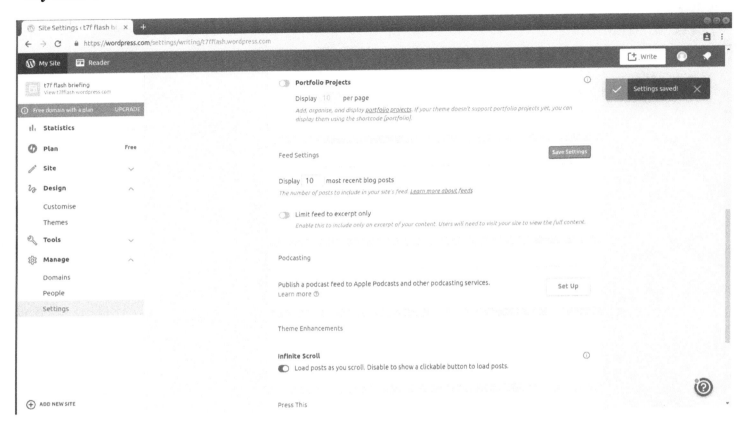

Chapter 5

Create some content on your WordPress.com site

You have created your site, now we need something for Alexa to read once we a have joined the site to the Flash Briefing skill.

At this point we need to make sure we have verified your email account. WordPress.com will have sent you an email to make sure you are not one of those robots that get everywhere. Have a look in your email and look for something titled "Activate [your website name]", click into the email and click the "Click here to Confirm Now".

You will then receive another email from WordPress.com asking you to log in again click this link and log in using the email address and password you set in the earlier section.

Click on the arrow to the right of site and then posts.

Now click on "**Add a New Post**".

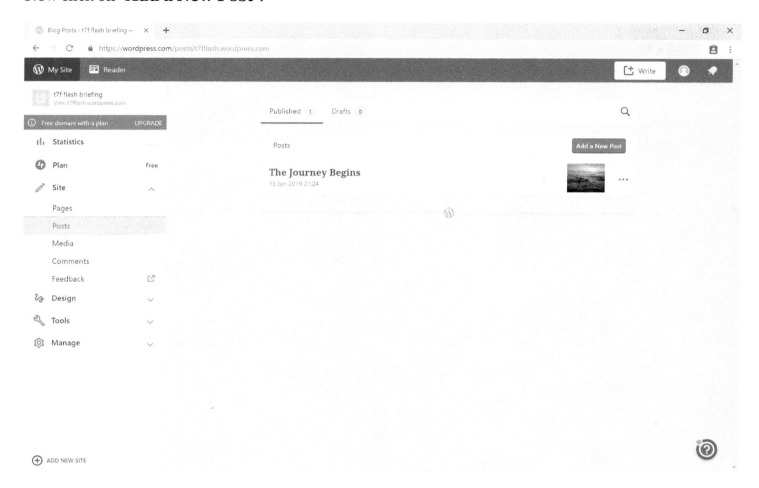

Here we have the page to create your first blog post.

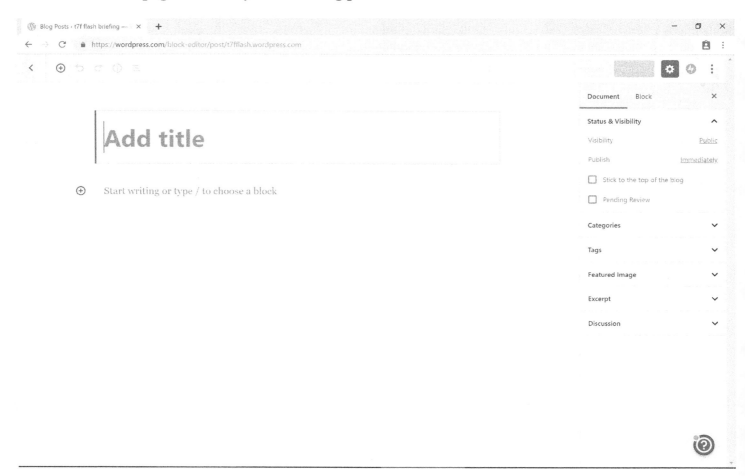

You can type whatever you like and give it whatever title you like. Just click through the help dialogues from WordPress.com.

When you have finished it should look like this, with maybe a few more words.

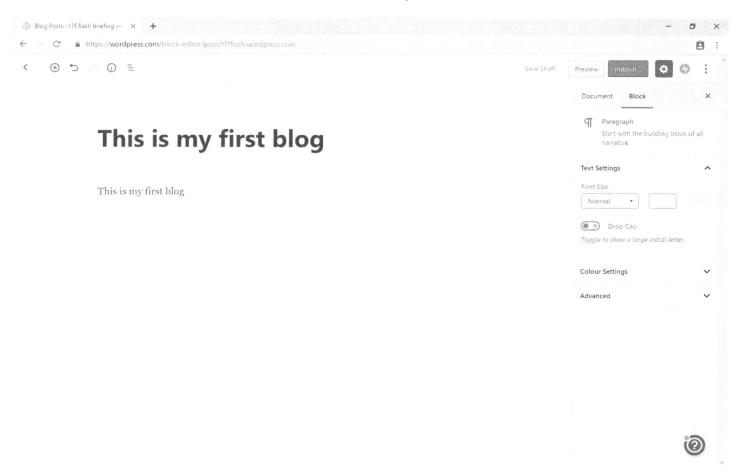

A note about RSS

I thought I would give a bit of background at this point as the next step might seem a little clunky :-).

The technology we are using to connect your WordPress.com site to the Alexa Skills Kit is called RSS which stands for Rich Site Summary or Really Simple Syndication and is widely used on the internet to allow sharing of information, especially for blogs.

RSS is a standardised format for websites to let other sites to find and access the information on their site. The format uses a way of identifiying different types of data within the content this method is called tags. A tag is define by and openign and closing less than and greater than sign "<>" in between is the name of the tag. The two tags we are concerned with are:

- the <content> tag which has the full information about your blog post.

- the <description> tag which is used for summary data of your blog post (often called an excerpt) and if not explicitly defined it is automatically populated by WordPress.com from the content part of your blog post but may not contain the whole of your post depending on the it's length.

In their infinite wisdom, Amazon has chosen to use the <description> instead of the <content> tag for the flash briefing skills so we need to force our content into the <description> tag.

Fortunately is it pretty straightforward, if not elegant.

Click on the **"Documents"** menu item of your blog post.

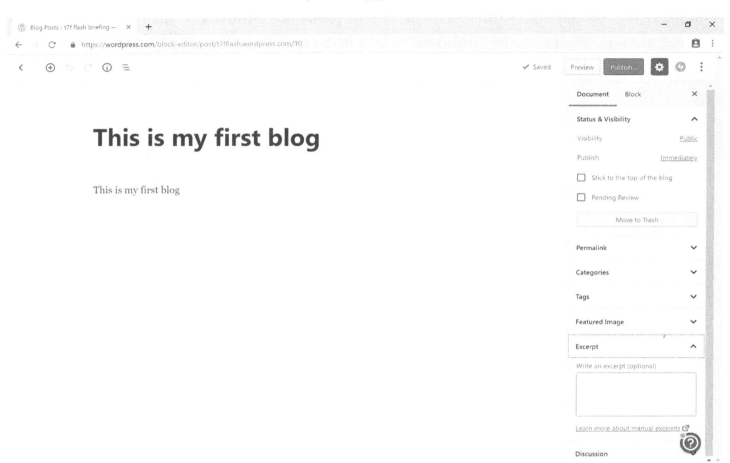

Select the text you have created for the body of your blog post and copy it into the **"Excerpt"** box on the right. You will need to do this for all of your posts, this ensures that the right information is passed to Alexa. Then click the **"Publish"** button in the top right.

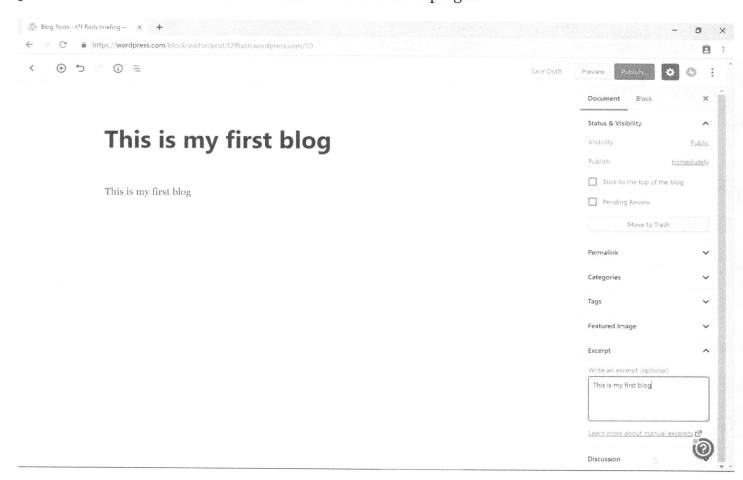

And click the **"Publish"** button again, we will talk about the scheduling capability in Appendix B.

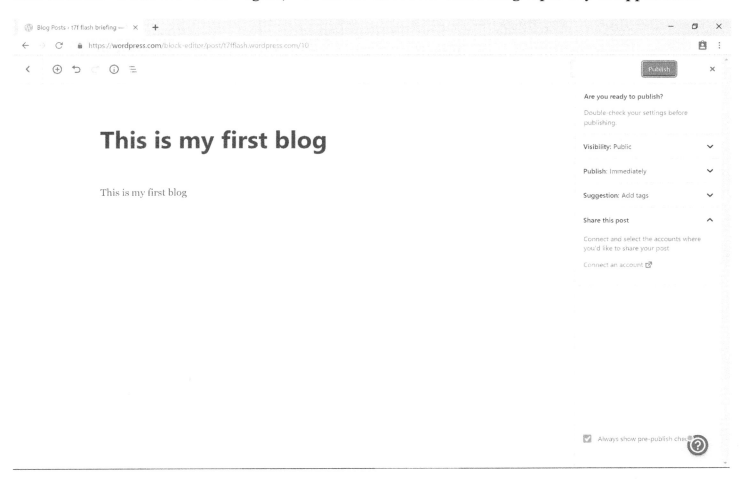

Congratulations, you have your first post live.

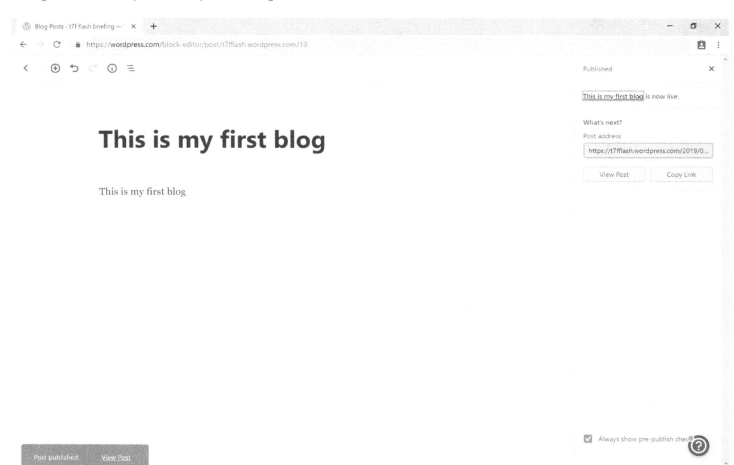

Just one little thing to complete, click the arrow button on the top left, when you hover over it it says "**View Posts**".

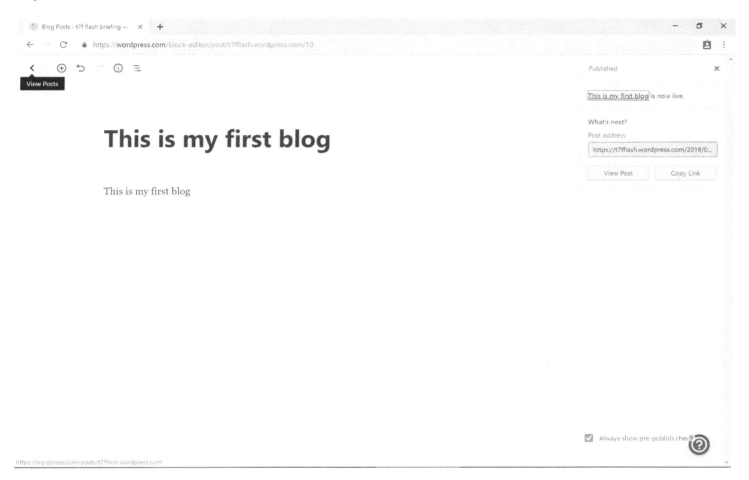

In the list of posts you will a post with the title "The Journey Begins." Do you remember doing that? Nah! WordPress.com pre-populates a first post to help people get started, we need to rid ourselves of it.

Click on the three dots to the right of it and a context menu will appear, click "**Bin**," you will get a message saying it has been moved to the trash.

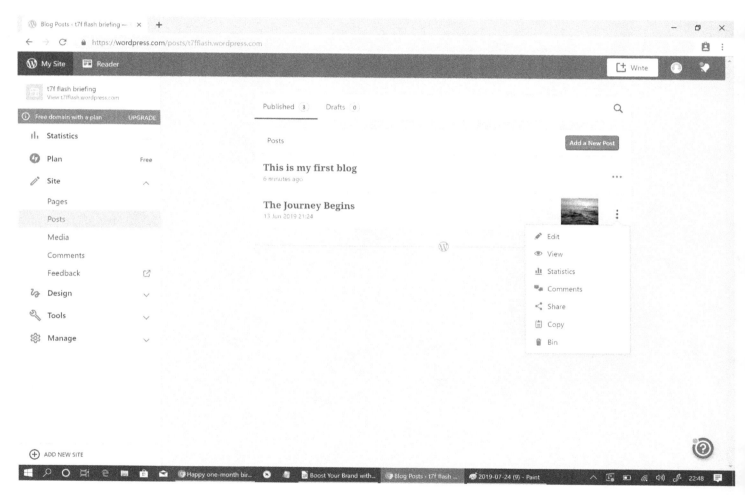

You will see we only have 1 post there. Don't worry about the count next to Published, that will update when you revisit this view in future. That's it your first post ready, now its time to connect it to Alexa.

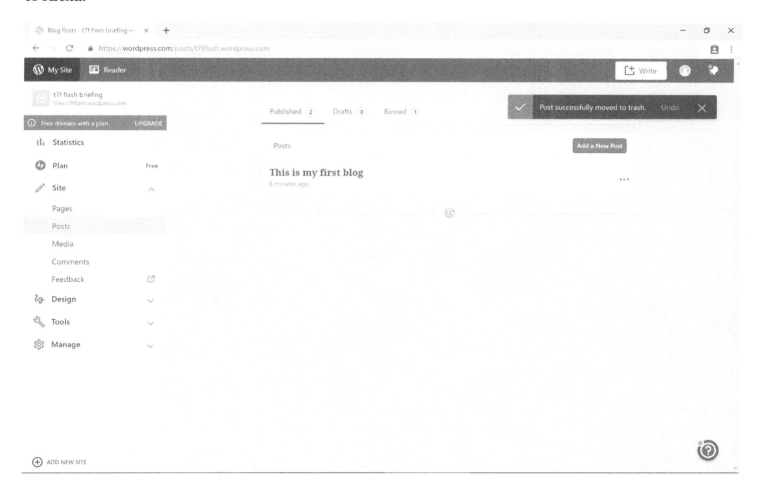

Chapter 6

Create your Flash Briefing Skill

Now that we have our WordPress.com site ready and our content published we will be able to get Alexa to use it. Reopen the tab in your browser that has the https://developer.amazon.com page or open a new tab and login with your email address and password you set up in Chapter 2.

Click on **"Developer Console"** at the top right.

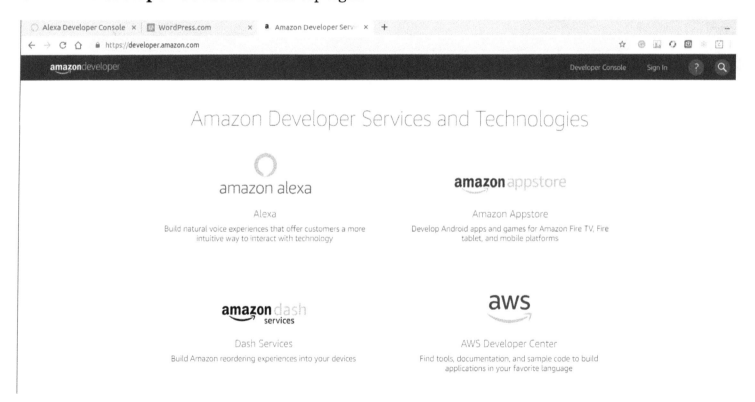

Click on "**Alexa**" and then "**Alexa Skills Kit**".

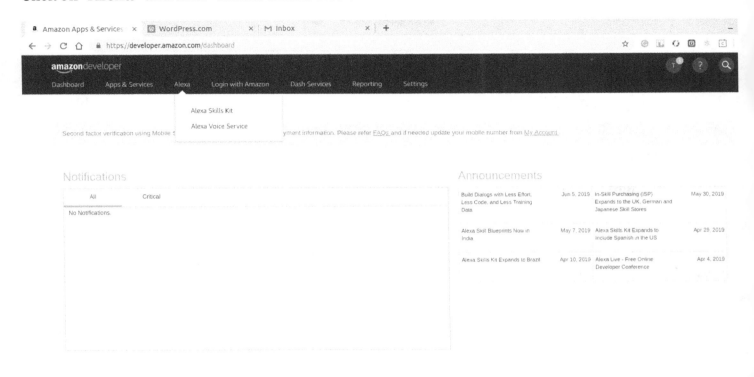

Click on **"Create Skill".**

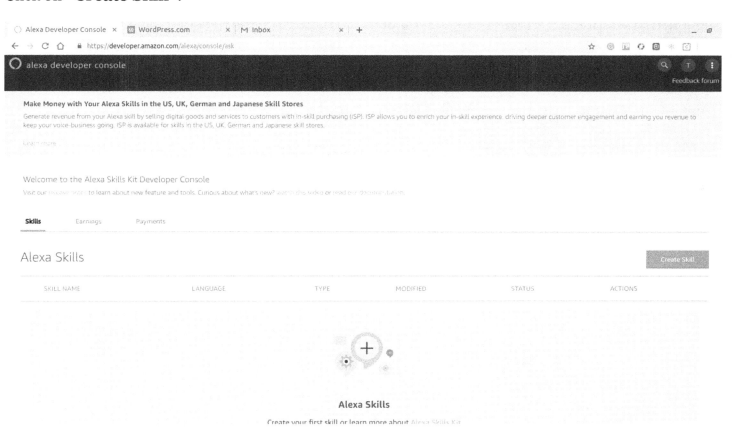

This where we name your skill and decide which country it will be available in. If you want to publish to multiple regions you can but you need to create a separate skill for each country.

So enter your preferred name of your skill, this is the name that will appear in the Alexa App and Amazon Store. Choose your preferred region. As you can see the selected type of skill to be created defaults to Custom, we obviously want Flash Briefing, so click on the **"Flash Briefing"** box.

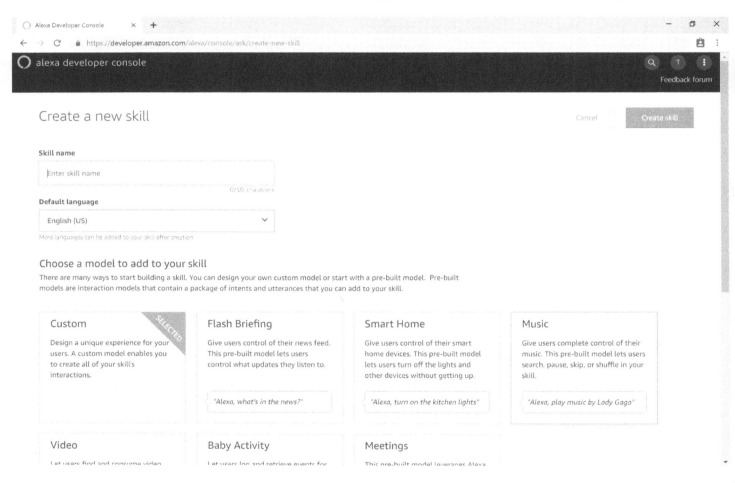

Click on the **"Create skill"** button on the top right.

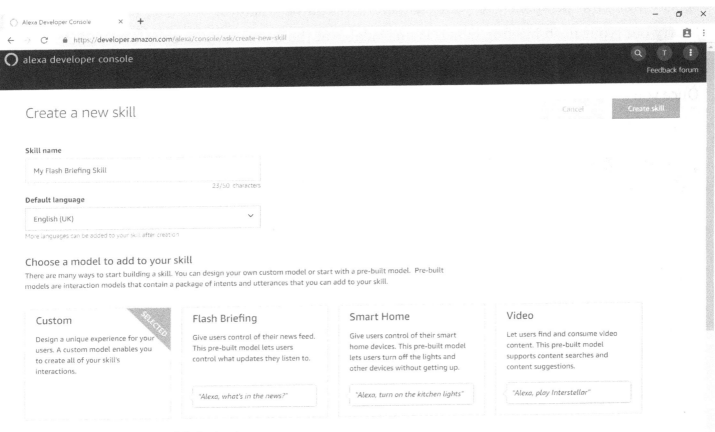

If for some reason there is a problem with Alexa accessing the WordPress.com feed we need to specify what will be spoken to your customer. It can be whatever you like, but something like, "Sorry but [your flash briefing name] is unavailable at the moment, please try later". Click the play button to see what it sounds like.

Once you are happy, click on the **"Add New Feed"** link below the message box.

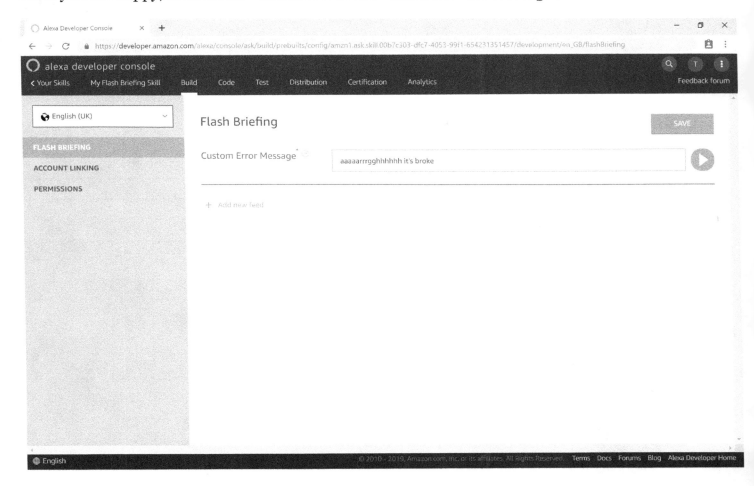

You now need to fill in each of these fields.

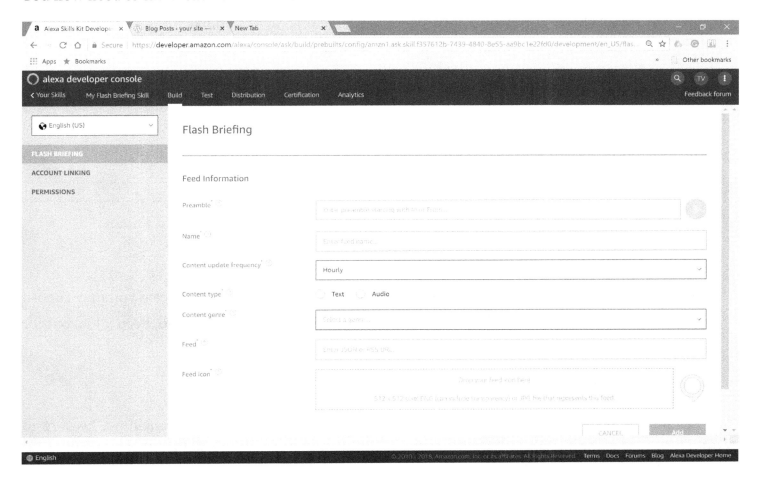

Below is an explanation of each of the fields:

Preamble

The preamble will be played every time your skill is used so you might want to use something like

- from [your skill name] or [your business name]

- in the latest news from [your skill name] or [your business name]

Play around with it, there are some restrictions but Amazon will tell you if it does not fit the conditions. Again click the play button to get a feel for what it will sound like.

Name

Within each flash briefing you can have multiple feeds so each needs a unique name, for our purposes we are only using 1 feed, but if you have several parts of your business you want to be able to publish flash briefings for under the same banner, you can do.

Content Update Frequency

This shows how often Alexa checks the feed has new content, I suggest leaving at 1 hour.

Content Type

Set this to text as we only have text within our feed. If you were to have a podcast you may choose the audio button but for now, let's stick with text. If you are interested in audio, keep a lookout for a future book specifically on the subject from me.

Content Genre

From the drop-down choose which category suits the information you are providing, be sure to think about it carefully as this is how Amazon groups together similar skills when customers are searching for them.

Feed

Now, this is where we get to the most important part. This is where we tell Amazon to look at your WordPress.com site. In here we want the URL of your site plus the addition of '/**feed**/'.

Your WordPress.com site is visible on the internet to people as something like t7fflash.wordpress.com, if you cannot remember what you called it, open up the WordPress.com tab we used to set up the site, if you do remember you can skip the next few steps.

Click on "**My site**". I have highlighted the part of the URL that you need to copy everything that is after '**/day/**'. Just highlight the equivalent of yours click you right mouse button and select copy.

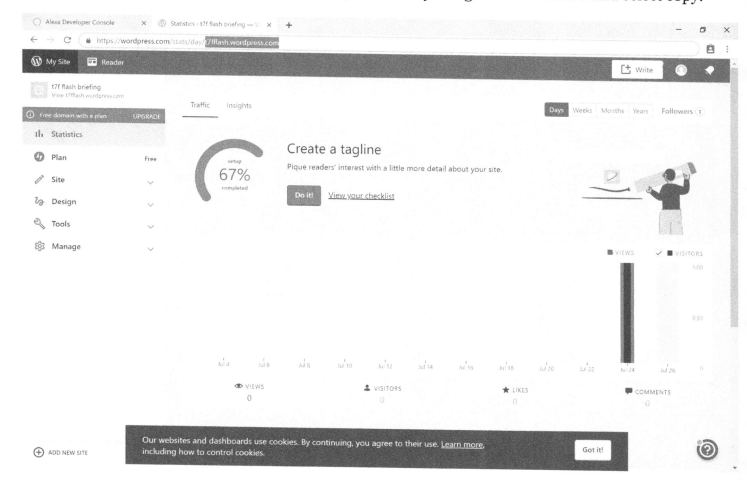

Paste the URL you copied into the feed box, you will see that it says invalid URL, you need to add '**https://**' to the beginning of it, we need to add '**/feed/**' to the end.

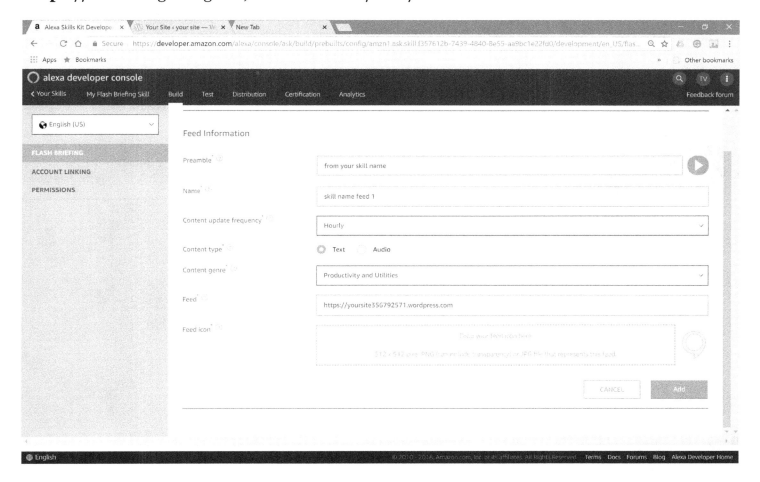

Feed Icon

This needs to be a 512 x 512 pixel image in either .jpg or .png format which represents your skill or brand. Click on the box and a file browser will pop up for you to choose the file that you are going to use.

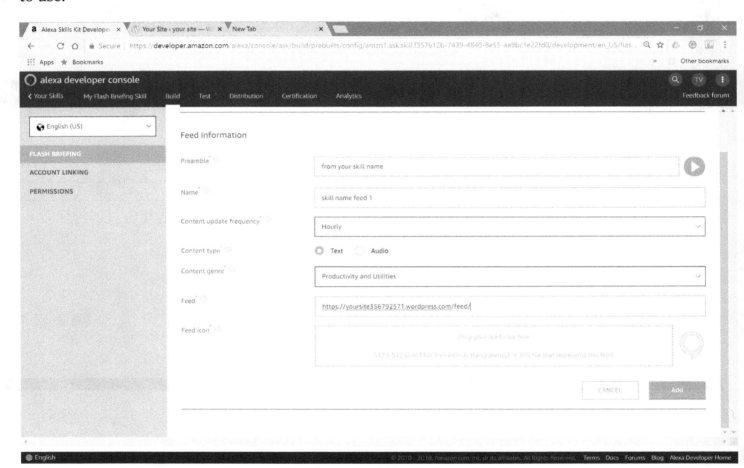

Now click on the "**Add**" button bottom right.

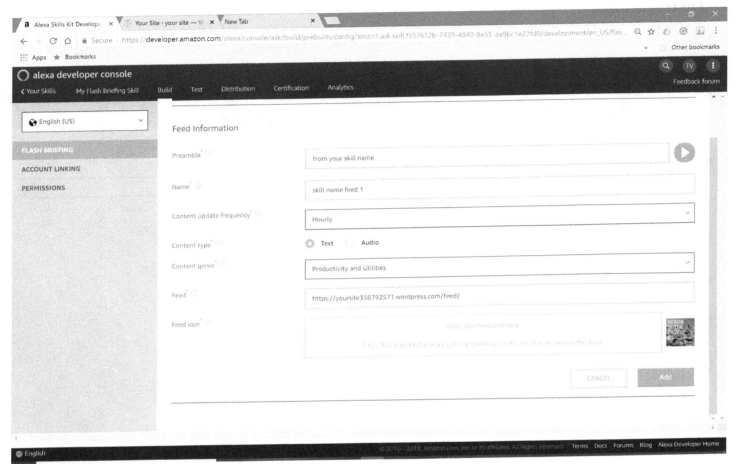

We have linked the skill to the blog, now we need to save it, so click "**Save**". Then click
"**Distribution**".

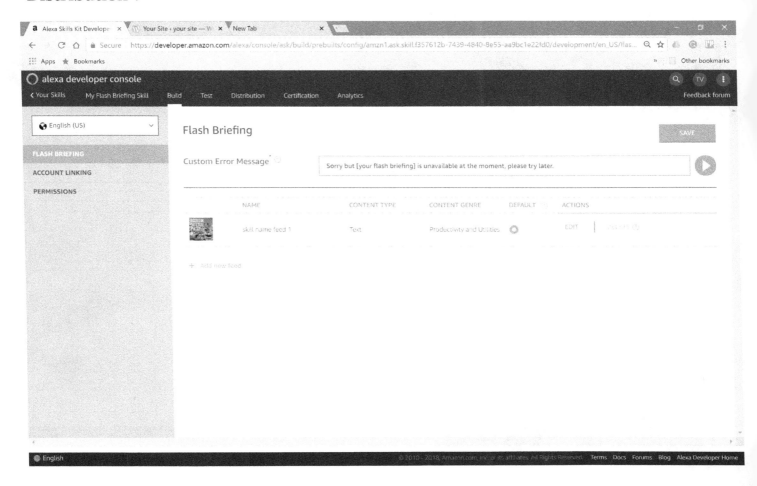

The reason we skip the Test tab is because at present the standard testing tool in the Alexa Skills Kit
does not support Flash Briefings, you can, however, use a product called echoism.io to test it.
Details on this are in Appendix B, and I have not included them in the body of this book as it is not
critical to run through the tests as the flash briefing is pretty simple.

Distribution

This page contains some key elements from a promotional point of view. This allows your skill to reach your intended audience. I advise using all of the available text, but think about making it punchy and really appealing to the audience so they enable your skill. Remember they are essentially deciding whether to invite you into their home every day to talk to them, make it compelling.

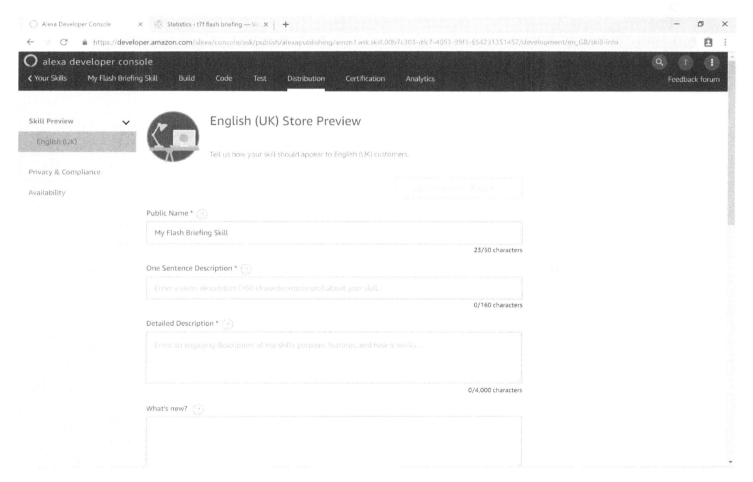

One Sentence Description: explain what's in it for the customer in a succinct manner.

Detailed Description: if they are reading this then your one sentence description has hooked them but they are not convinced, convince them.

What's New: this is only needed if you make updates to the skill in the future so you can leave this blank for now.

Category: again choose the classification that suits your brand and skill

Small Icon & Large Icon: Use the same one we used earlier the 512 and a scaled down one for the small icon.

Keywords: this is potentially a whole book on its own. You may have heard of Search Engine Optimisation and similar phrases, well the keywords are one of the things that Amazon's search engine uses to decide what to show to someone when they look for something in their store. If you have a skill that is to do with fishing and do not have the words "fishing" or "lake" or "angling", then you will miss out on your target market. Thinking about who you want to hit could take you ages so I suggest trying a few, you can always add and remove later on.

Privacy Policy & Terms of Use: if the nature of the information you are providing needs some disclaimer or limitations of use e.g. if it was financial advice.

Once you are happy with all the content click **"Save and continue"**.

In this section select **"No"** to all items, unless you think they really apply, then click the **"Export Compliance"** checkbox.

Scroll down and in the Testing Instructions box just put **"Simple Flash briefing with one feed"** into specific instructions. Then click **"Save and Continue"**.

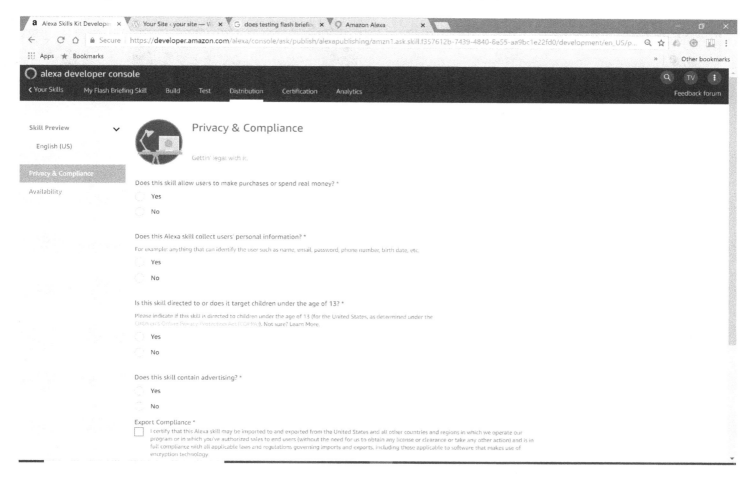

On this page just click **"Save and continue"**, unless you have some specific countries you do not want the skill available in. If you do want to restrict it click on "**Selected countries and regions**" radio button and make your selections and then click **"Save and continue"**.

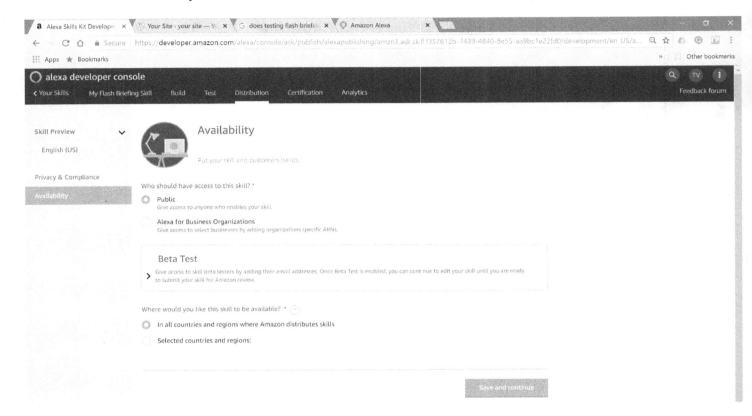

The Validation tests run automatically and you should have no errors, if you have some then go back to the relevant page and make corrections. Click on **"Functional test"**.

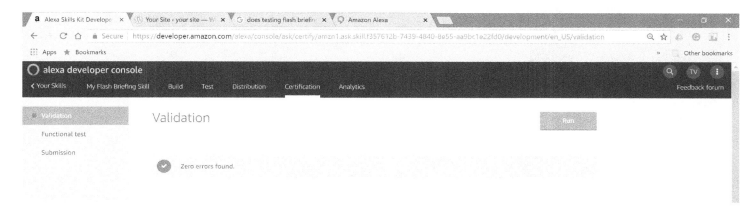

Click **"Run"**.

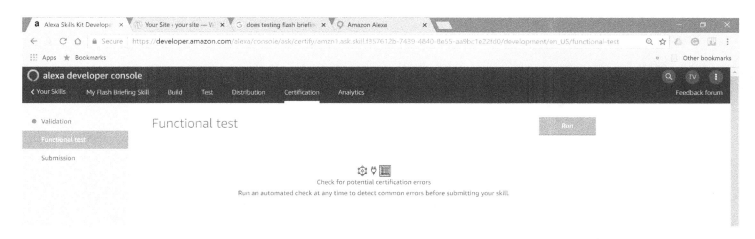

It may take a minute or two to test but you should see:

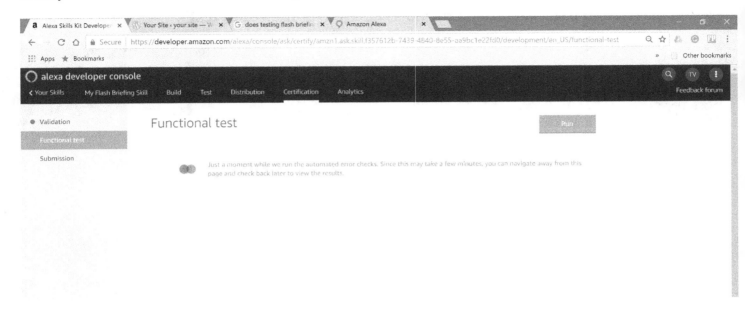

Once you see zero errors found, click on **"Submission"**. If there are errors have a look at the information and again make the relevant corrections.

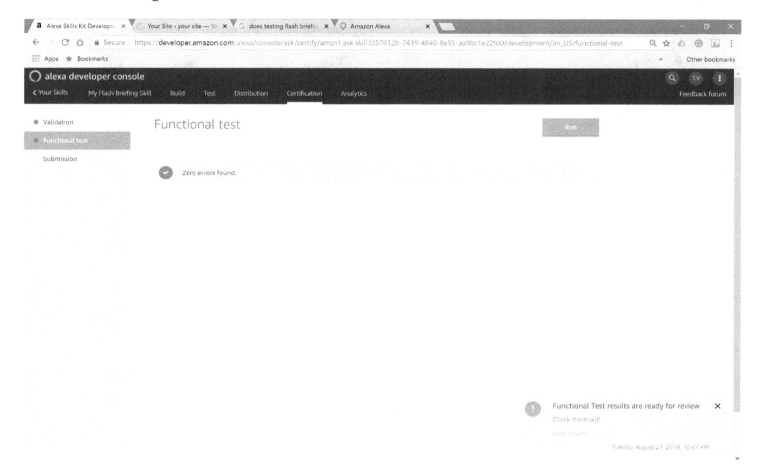

Click on **"Submit for review"**.

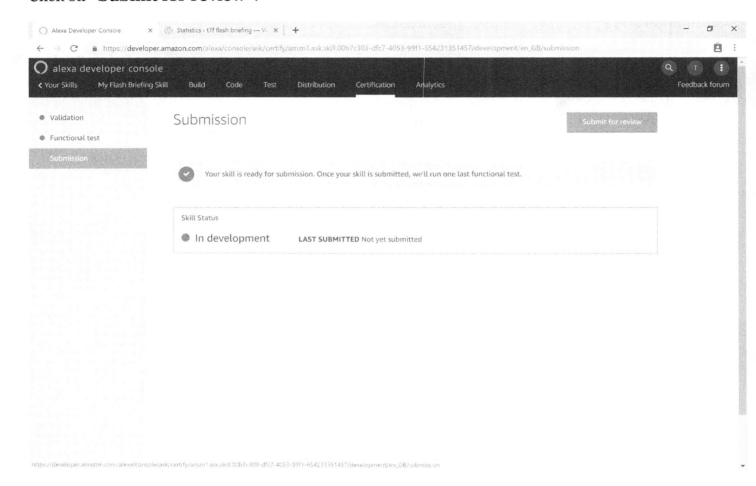

This page will display while the submission process happens.

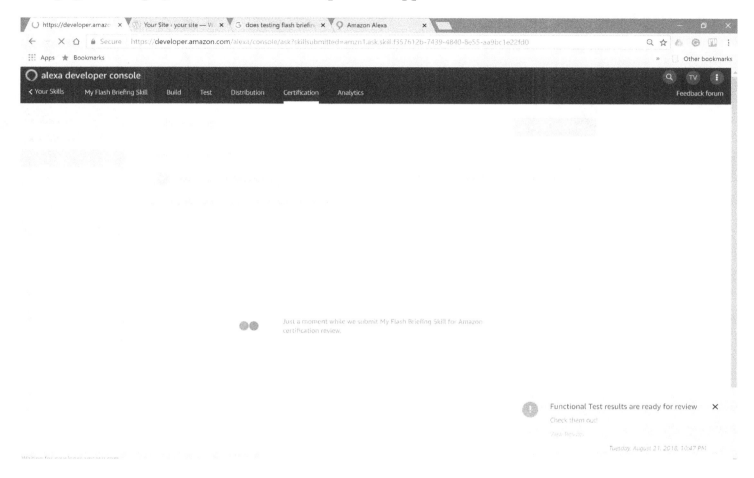

You should now see this screen, that's it, you have created your first skill and submitted it to the Amazon review engine.

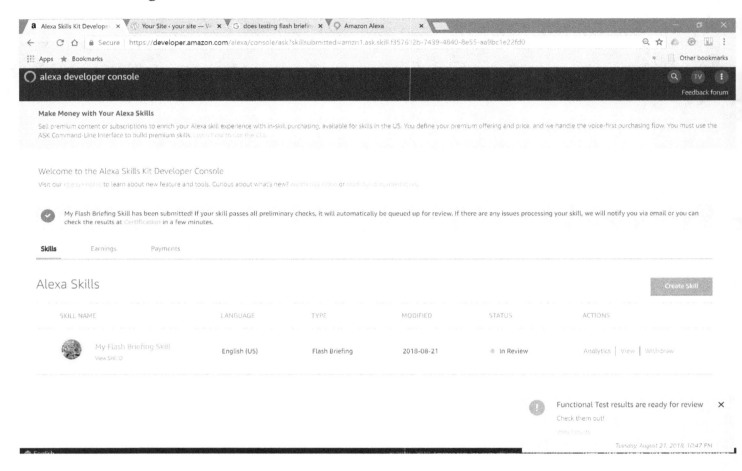

You should now also receive an email similar to the one below.

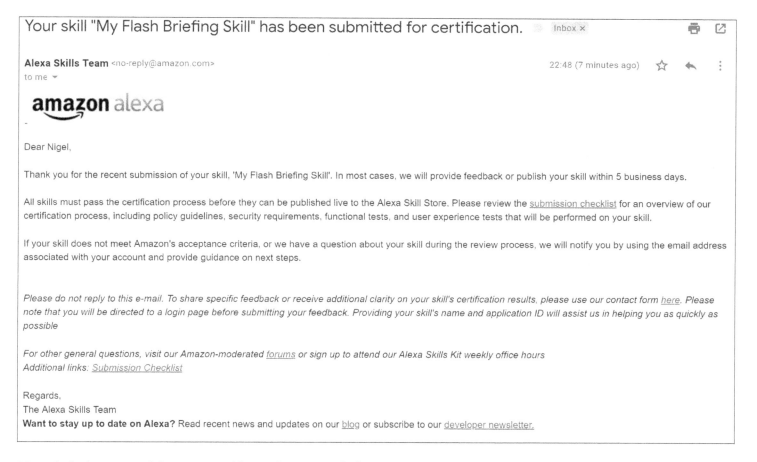

Now it is just a waiting game, if you have used the same email address for your Amazon Developer account as the one your own Echo device is registered with, you will be able to enable to the skill in its 'dev' state, if not you will have wait on Amazon review team.

My experience is that they turn around the Flash Briefing ones pretty quick and the only issue I had was when I had no content on the WordPress.com site.

If there is something that Amazon is not happy about you may get an email like this. If you do just make the tweaks needed and resubmit.

Certification feedback for your Alexa skill My Flash Briefing Skill

no-reply-skilldev@amazon.com <no-reply-skilldev@amazon.com>   12:29 (1 hour ago)
to me ▾

Dear Nigel,

Thank you for the recent submission of your My Flash Briefing Skill Content skill.

Unfortunately, your skill has not been published on Amazon Alexa.

Your skill appears to be a test or only intended for personal use.

If you think you have received this message in error, resubmit your skill for certification and clarify in the testing instructions how this skill is not a test skill.

Please note that this is a test skill based on the skill's response and description.

To learn more about how to submit your skill, read our getting started guide or check out an introduction to the Alexa skills kit on our blog. We look forward to seeing what you create.

Please do not reply to this e-mail. To share specific feedback or receive additional clarity on your skill's certification results, please use our contact form here.Please note that you will be directed to a login page before submitting your feedback.Providing your skill's name and application ID will assist us in helping you as quickly as possible.

...estions, visit our Amazon-moderated forums or sign up to attend our Alexa Skills Kit weekly office hours.

When they have reviewed it you will get an email similar to this, and then its a case of promoting the skill through whatever channels you use.

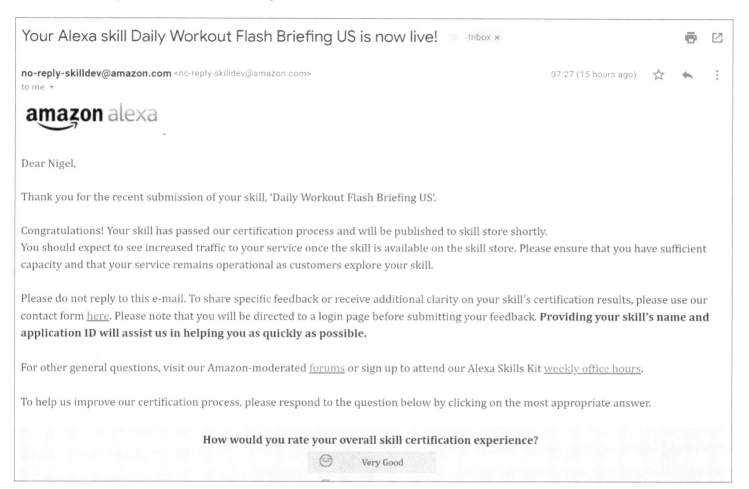

Chapter 7

Conclusion

I hope you have found this guide useful, and will keep it as a handy reminder for each new skill you create. If it has whetted your appetite to do more, as it did with me when I had a go at my first skill, then keep an eye out on Amazon for further simple guides from me. This skill is literally the tip, of the tip, of the tip, of the tip of the iceberg when it comes to what can be done with the Alexa Skills Kit.

Appendix A
Scheduling Posts

I mentioned earlier that I would talk about how to schedule a post. I am not going to go back over the instructions from the earlier part of the book so make you follow the instructions together. (e.g. don't forget to paste your post content into the excerpt section.) Open your WordPress.com site. And click on **"Site"** and **"Posts"** then click **"Add a New Post"** on the following page.

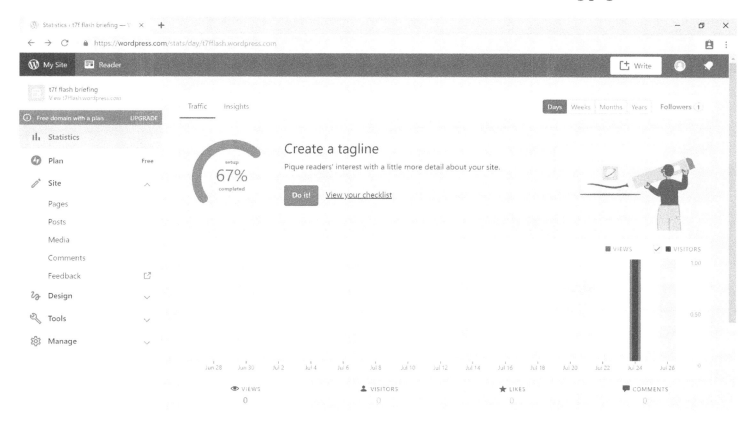

On this page enter the content you want Alexa to say.

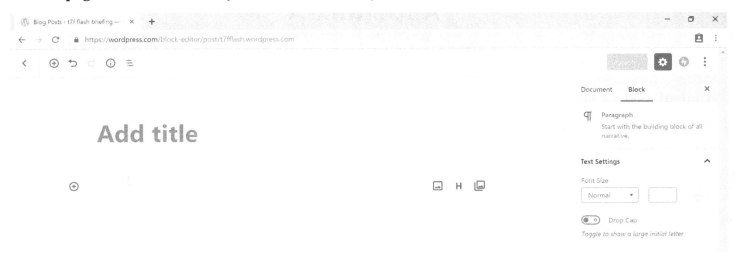

When you are happy with what you want her to say then click on the **"Publish"** button in the top right.

Click on the arrow to the right of where it says **"Publish: Immediately"**.

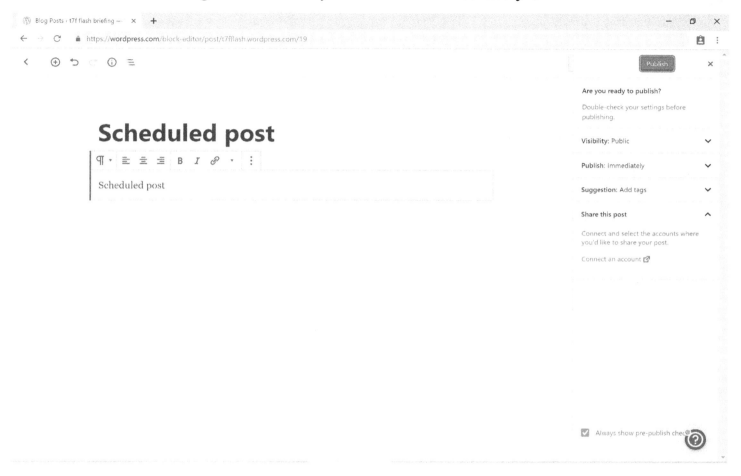

Choose the date and time you want your post to be available. Then click the **"Publish"** button.

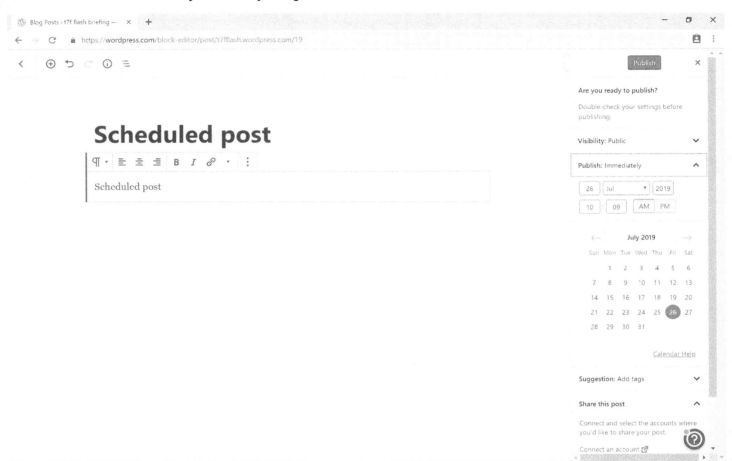

You should see this message confirming the date and time you selected. Click on the arrow next to the plus in a circle on the left of the screen, not the browser back button.

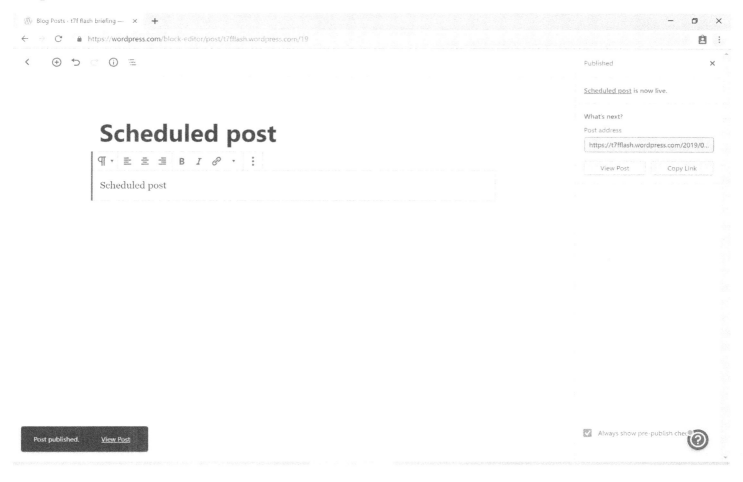

You will see there is now a number 1 next to the **"Scheduled"** tab, click on it.

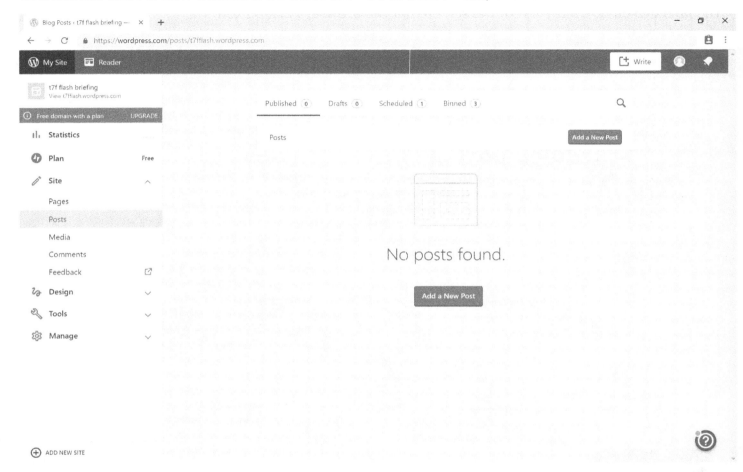

There we go, this is the post you created and if you look under the title it says when it will be published, in this case in 14 hours. You can now go ahead and create and schedule as many as you want. This is exactly the approach I use for one of my skills.

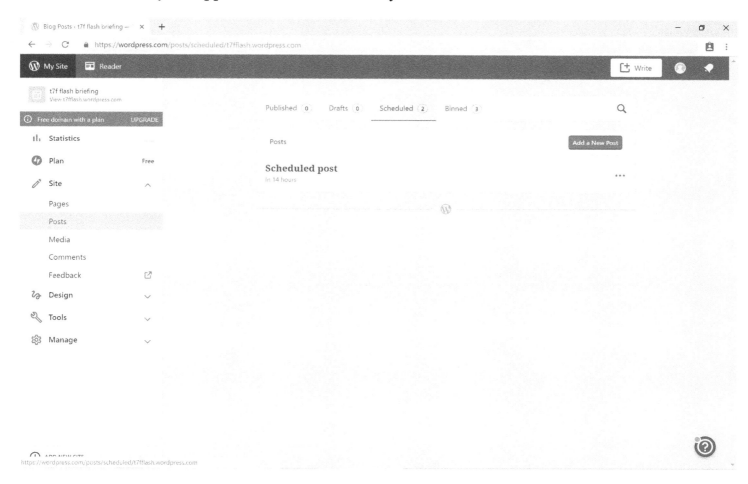

Appendix B

Testing with Echoism.io

As I mentioned earlier in the book at the time of writing the flash briefing skills are not able to be tested using the Amazon Skills Kit tool but you can use another tool called echoism.io.

Enable your skill

Before we can start using echoism.io we need to make sure your skill is enabled for the Amazon account you are going to use.

Open a new tab in your browser and go to https://alexa.amazon.com and login using your development account. Click on **"Skills"**.

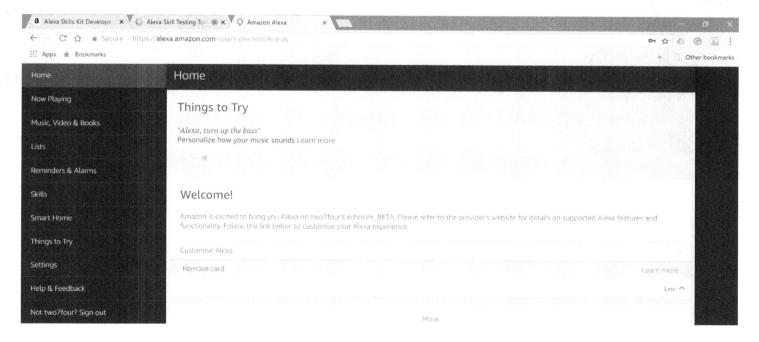

Click on **"Your Skills"**, you should see the following:

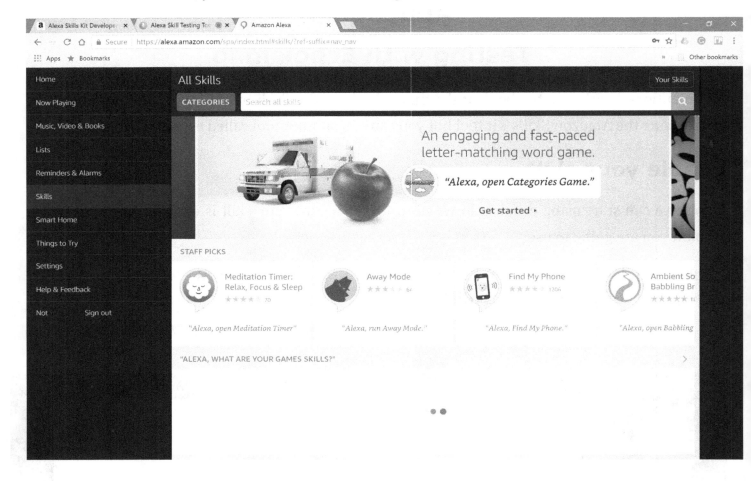

Click on the **"skill name"** you created earlier.

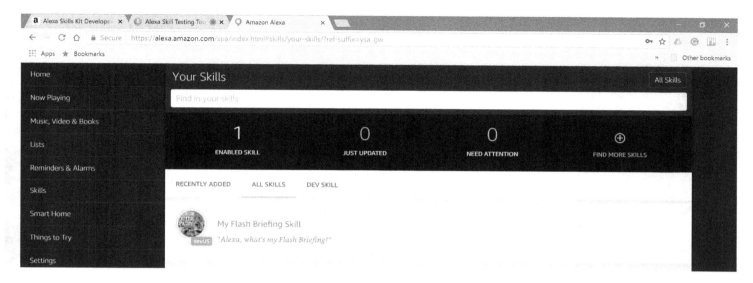

Click **"Settings"**.

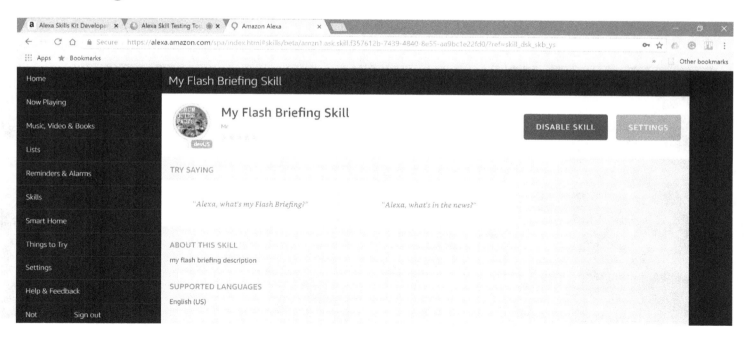

Click **"Manage Flash Briefings"**.

Make sure your feed is set to **"On"**.

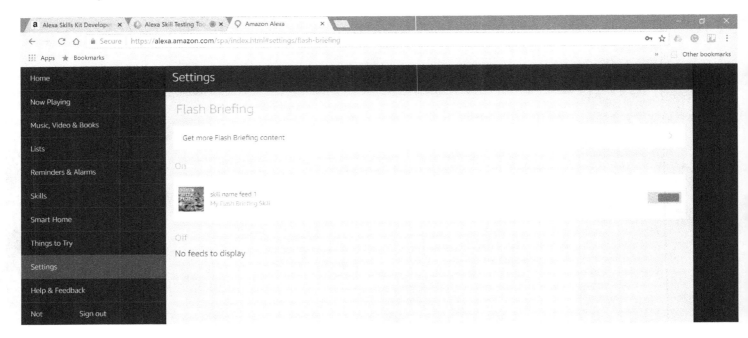

Connect Echosim.io to your Developer Account

Open a new tab in your browser and type in www.echoism.io.

Click **"Login with Amazon"**. Use the account you used to create your skill as a login.

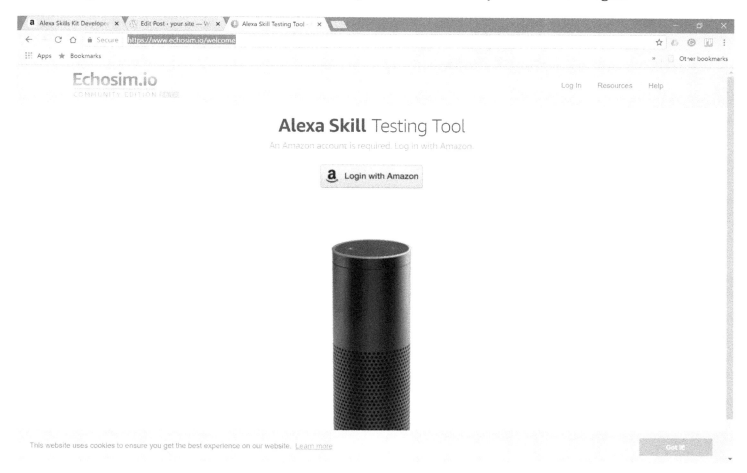

Click **"Allow"**.

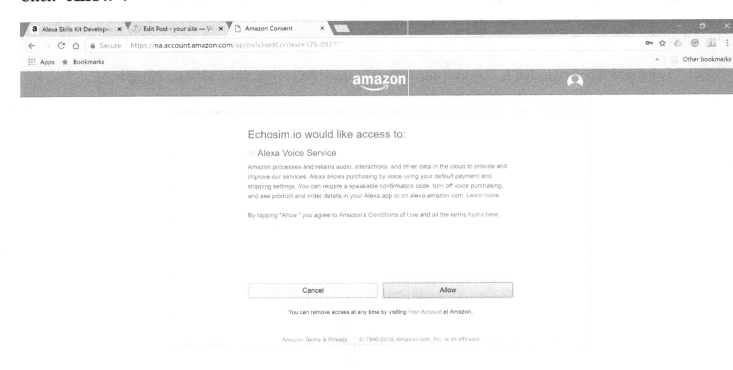

To use the virtual device you either hold your space bar down and speak to Alexa or use your mouse to click on the microphone logo. Make sure you have a microphone enabled on the device you are using and the speaker volume up. Then just say "Alexa, what's my flash briefing."

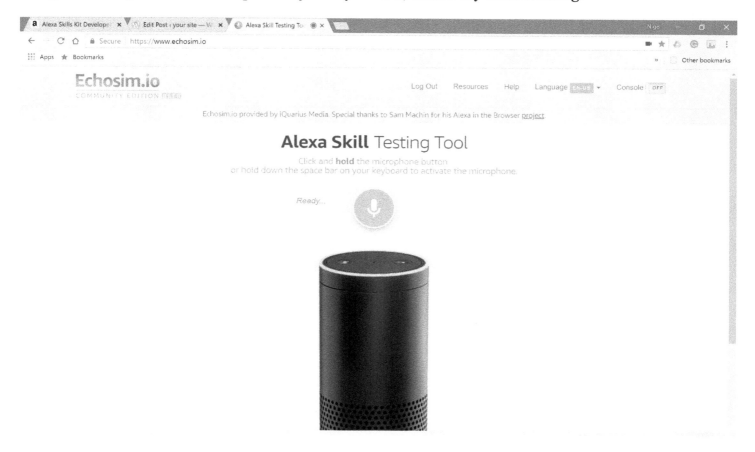

Appendix C

In the production of this guide I have been experimenting with a number of Alexa skills, below are a couple of examples. For more examples visit www.two7four.com/digital.

Daily Workout Flash Briefing

 I include this one first as it was the one that inspired the production of this book. Each day, through the flash briefing a varied short workout is read out by Alexa.

www.two7four.com/dailyworkout

My Local Flash Briefing

 This is my latest skill using the technique I provide in this guide. With this skill I have different feeds from different pubs and customers can subscribe to the ones they are interested in. Each pub has their own blog and just update it when they want to.

www.two7four.com/mylocal

Appendix X

So one out of two is not bad, you are obviously curious. Now back to the instructions, please. Tut! Tut! :-) Only joking.

Dedication

To my beautiful wife and daughters who have no idea what I do for a living. They have as much knowledge as the characters in friends do about Chandler's job. So I just say I am a transponster.

Also By Nigel Creaser

Available Now

Check out www.nigelcreaser.com/sundaylunchpm for more information.

When I Were a Project Manager

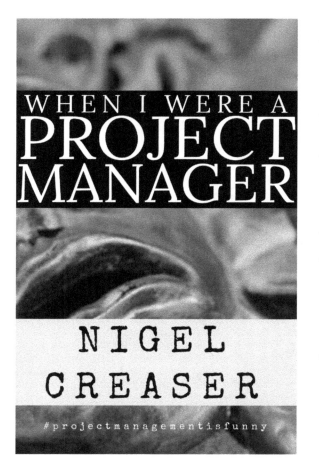

Where it all began.

Are you a new project manager wondering what life might be like at the end of your career, maybe reminiscing about the journey with colleagues? Do you want a tiny glimpse into your future?

Are you an accomplished project manager who recognises the funny stuff in the life of a project manager?

Well, this is the book for you! A parody of the "Four Yorkshiremen" sketch adapted for the project management community.

Peter Taylor, author of The Lazy Project Manager says:

"Python meets Project Manager! As a Monty Python fan and Lazy Project Manager, I just loved this excellent reworking"

Pick it up here www.nigelcreaser.com/shop.

Project Management: The Sketches

This book has been described in many ways, *"..-.I laughed so hard I nearly peed my pants."*

"This book single-handedly help me pass my PMP, APM, Prince 2 and grade 3 bassoon exams."

"...the funniest book on Project Management I have ever read."

"Well, it made me laugh."

None of these statements have been said about it, except the first one, Peter Taylor, The Lazy Project Manager said that and he is in the book. Blast, no not the first one, the last one, yeah the last one, that's what he said.

What would happen if all comedy sketches were about project management? Wouldn't that be great? Not sure? Well, no need to worry. You no longer have to imagine it, here is a collection of twelve, yes count them, twelve comedy sketches and songs all about project management.

Through these twelve chapters, you will continue to follow the formative days in project management of our intrepid hero George Onaswell. You will have a fly on the wall view of his is trials, his tribulations and the characters that shaped his project management career.

Pick it up here www.nigelcreaser.com/shop.

Coming Soon

Project Management: The Interviews

Interviews with the great and the good of the project management world, from Lazy to Digital to the Doctor.

Sign up to the mailing list to get early notification of the release date www.nigelcreaser.com/mailinglist .

The Sunday Lunch Project

George Onaswell is a typical Project Manager, and has been delivering projects for years, adept stakeholder manager and Gantt chart guru, then he gets the most terrifying high profile project of his career! Cooking Sunday lunch for his prospective mother-in-law, head of the local Women's Institute and national roast dinner of the year champion four years on the trot.

How can he make it a roaring success while still delivering the thorny project he just got landed in the office?

The project charter is drafted for . . . .

The Sunday Lunch Project!!!

What could possibly go wrong?

In all good book-stores (and rubbish ones) in 2020 (...or in that general regionish)

About the Author

Nigel Creaser, PMP, PMQ, PSM is an experienced project and programme manager with over 20 years of varied project management roles, delivering multi-million pound projects across a wide range of industries including national and regional government, financial services and telecoms and a former Director of Marketing for the Project Management Institute's UK Chapter.

He lives in North Shropshire with his wife and two daughters. When he is not mangling projects or being a husband and dad you can find him on a judo mat trying to stay standing or running around trying to get a bit faster and running a little bit further.

To get the latest updates why not pop along to www.nigelcreaser.com or sign up to the newsletter here www.nigelcreaser.com/mailinglist.

www.ingramcontent.com/pod-product-compliance
Lightning Source LLC
Chambersburg PA
CBHW080537060326
40690CB00022B/5163